The Holy Sabbath
A Covenant for God's People

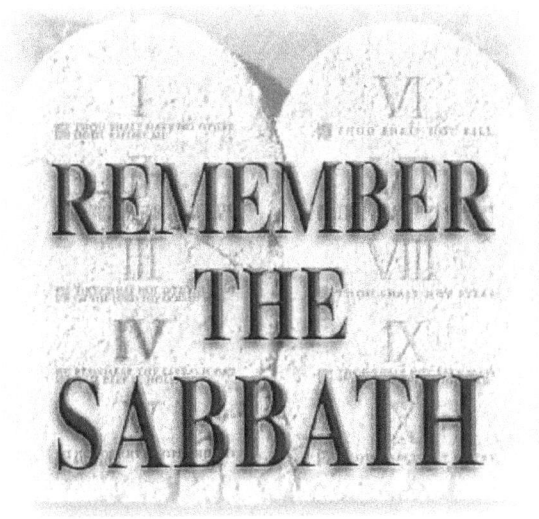

By Karajah Yashar

BLACKSTONE PUBLISHING

Orlando, FL

The Holy Sabbath
A Covenant for God's People

www.bspbooks.com

ISBN: 978-1-962691-30-7

First Edition: June 2024

Table of Contents:

Chapter One: A Sacred Rhythm

The sun began to set over the ancient hills of Judea, casting a golden hue over the city of Jerusalem. As the shadows lengthened, the bustling marketplace gradually quieted, and the people of Israel prepared for the most sacred time of their week: the Sabbath.

"Remember the sabbath day, to keep it holy. Six days shalt thou labour, and do all thy work: But the seventh day is the sabbath of the Lord thy God: in it thou shalt not do any work, thou, nor thy son, nor thy daughter, thy manservant, nor thy maidservant, nor thy cattle, nor thy stranger that is within thy gates" (Exodus 20:8-10).

As the final preparations were made, families gathered in their homes, lighting the Sabbath candles and reciting blessings that had been passed down through generations. This day of rest, ordained by God at the dawn of creation, was not only a respite from labor but a celebration of their covenant with the Almighty.

"Thus the heavens and the earth were finished, and all the host of them. And on the seventh day God ended his work which he had made; and he rested on the seventh day from all his work which he had made. And God blessed the seventh day, and

sanctified it: because that in it he had rested from all his work which God created and made" (Genesis 2:1-3).

The Sabbath in Israel

The Israelites understood the Sabbath as more than a ritualistic practice; it was a divine ordinance that set them apart from other nations. It was a day of reflection, worship, and communal bonding, reinforcing their identity as God's chosen people. The Torah had detailed the Sabbath's observance, embedding it deeply into the fabric of their lives.

During the time of Nehemiah, after the return from Babylonian exile, the importance of the Sabbath was emphatically reinforced. Nehemiah, recognizing the spiritual neglect that had led to Israel's downfall, took decisive measures to restore its sanctity.

"In those days saw I in Judah some treading wine presses on the sabbath, and bringing in sheaves, and lading asses; as also wine, grapes, and figs, and all manner of burdens, which they brought into Jerusalem on the sabbath day: and I testified against them in the day wherein they sold victuals" (Nehemiah 13:15).

His reforms were strict, yet necessary, to remind the people of their covenantal obligations. Nehemiah's actions were a clarion call to honor the Sabbath, to resist the encroachments of secular activities, and to recommit to the divine rhythm established by God.

The Sabbath and the Church of Christ

Centuries later, in a small, burgeoning community within the Roman Empire, the early Christians faced a similar challenge of maintaining their distinct identity amidst a world that often ignored sacred times of rest. For the followers of Christ, the Sabbath took on an enriched meaning.

"And he said unto them, The sabbath was made for man, and not man for the sabbath: Therefore the Son of man is Lord also of the sabbath" (Mark 2:27-28).

Jesus Christ, through His teachings and miracles, redefined the Sabbath's observance. His assertion of lordship over the Sabbath highlighted its true purpose—restorative and redemptive, a day for doing good and reflecting God's love.

In the book of Acts, the apostles continued to honor the Sabbath, gathering for worship and teaching. They met in synagogues and homes, breaking bread and sharing the good news of Jesus Christ.

"And Paul, as his manner was, went in unto them, and three sabbath days reasoned with them out of the scriptures" (Acts 17:2).

The early Church, acknowledged the traditional Sabbath keeping it a Holy and sanctified day.

A Timeless Ordinance

As the stars appeared in the night sky, twinkling over the serene landscape of Jerusalem, the world beyond remained oblivious to this sacred pause. Yet, within the hearts of those who kept the Sabbath, there was a profound peace, a sense of belonging to something greater than themselves. This sacred rhythm, established at the dawn of time, continued to echo through the ages, a testament to the divine order and a reminder of humanity's ultimate rest in God.

In our fast-paced, modern world, the call to remember the Sabbath resonates with renewed urgency. It beckons us to step out of the relentless cycle of work and consumption, to find rest and renewal in the presence of the Creator. It is a call to reconnect with the sacred, to honor the divine pattern of work and rest, and to embrace the peace that comes from knowing that we are part of God's eternal story.

"There remaineth therefore a rest to the people of God. For he that is entered into his rest, he also hath ceased from his own works, as God did from his" (Hebrews 4:9-10).

As we embark on this exploration of the Sabbath, let us journey through the Scriptures and the history of God's people, discovering anew the depth and beauty of this divine gift. Let us learn from the Israelites and the early Church of Christ, and let their faithfulness inspire us to keep the Sabbath holy, finding in it a source of strength, renewal, and divine communion.

Chapter Two:
A Covenant with God's People

The Sabbath stands as a unique and profound sign that sets God's people apart from the rest of the world. It is more than a day of rest; it is a covenant, a vow between God and His followers, marking them as distinct in their commitment to Him. This chapter explores the significance of the Sabbath as a distinguishing feature of God's people and its implications for believers today.

The Sabbath as a Covenant

The concept of the Sabbath as a covenantal sign is deeply rooted in Scripture. God established the Sabbath as a perpetual covenant between Himself and His people, symbolizing their special relationship.

"Wherefore the children of Israel shall keep the sabbath, to observe the sabbath throughout their generations, for a perpetual covenant. It is a sign between me and the children of Israel for ever: for in six days the Lord made heaven and earth, and on the seventh day he rested, and was refreshed" (Exodus 31:16-17).

This passage highlights the Sabbath as an everlasting sign of the covenant between God and the Israelites, a testament to their unique identity as His chosen people.

A Distinctive Mark of Faith

The Sabbath distinguishes God's people from others by their dedication to resting and worshipping on the seventh day. This practice sets them apart in a world that often values constant activity and productivity.

"Moreover also I gave them my sabbaths, to be a sign between me and them, that they might know that I am the Lord that sanctify them" (Ezekiel 20:12).

By observing the Sabbath, believers demonstrate their obedience to God's command and their trust in His sanctifying power. This act of faith serves as a visible sign of their commitment to Him and their willingness to live according to His ways.

A Countercultural Practice

In a society that frequently overlooks the need for rest and spiritual renewal, Sabbath observance is a countercultural practice. It challenges the norms of a busy world and proclaims a different set of values centered on God's provision and rest.

"And I will take you to me for a people, and I will be to you a God: and ye shall know that I am the Lord your God, which bringeth you out from under the burdens of the Egyptians" (Exodus 6:7).

Just as God delivered the Israelites from slavery in Egypt, He calls His people to step out of the relentless demands of daily life and enter into His rest. Observing the Sabbath becomes a declaration of freedom from the world's pressures and a commitment to God's kingdom.

A Sign of Holiness

The Sabbath is also a sign of holiness, reflecting God's own rest after creation and His desire for His people to share in that rest. By keeping the Sabbath, believers align themselves with God's holy purposes.

"Speak thou also unto the children of Israel, saying, Verily my sabbaths ye shall keep: for it is a sign between me and you throughout your generations; that ye may know that I am the Lord that doth sanctify you" (Exodus 31:13).

This sanctification process sets God's people apart, marking them as holy and dedicated to His service. The Sabbath, therefore, is not just a day of rest but a day of sanctification, reinforcing their identity as God's holy people.

Practical Implications for Believers

1. **Visible Testimony**: Observing the Sabbath serves as a visible testimony of a believer's faith and commitment to God. It sets them apart in their communities, showcasing their

dedication to divine principles over societal norms.

2. **Spiritual Renewal**: The Sabbath provides a regular opportunity for spiritual renewal, allowing believers to reconnect with God, reflect on His blessings, and realign their lives with His will.

3. **Community Strengthening**: As believers gather for worship and fellowship on the Sabbath, they strengthen their sense of community and shared purpose. This collective observance reinforces their identity as God's people.

4. **Rest and Reflection**: By setting aside one day for rest and reflection, believers acknowledge God's sovereignty and provision. It is a weekly reminder that their lives are in His hands, fostering a deep sense of peace and trust.

Chapter Three:
Who Should Keep the Sabbath?

The Sabbath is a day set apart by God for rest and worship, a commandment given not just to a specific group but to all of humanity. From its institution in Genesis to its reaffirmation to Israel, the Sabbath is a gift and a command that extends beyond ethnic and religious boundaries.

The Universal Origin of the Sabbath

The Sabbath's origin dates back to the creation of the world, indicating its universal significance for all humanity. In Genesis, God established the seventh day as a day of rest.

"And on the seventh day God ended his work which he had made; and he rested on the seventh day from all his work which he had made. And God blessed the seventh day, and sanctified it: because that in it he had rested from all his work which God created and made" (Genesis 2:2-3).

This passage shows that the Sabbath was instituted long before the formation of Israel as a nation. God blessed and sanctified the seventh day, setting a precedent for all of humanity to follow. It was a day meant for everyone to rest and reflect on God's creation and provision.

The Sabbath Commandment to Israel

While the Sabbath was instituted at creation, it was explicitly commanded to the Israelites as part of the Ten Commandments, reinforcing its importance.

"Remember the sabbath day, to keep it holy. Six days shalt thou labour, and do all thy work: But the seventh day is the sabbath of the Lord thy God: in it thou shalt not do any work, thou, nor thy son, nor thy daughter, thy manservant, nor thy maidservant, nor thy cattle, nor thy stranger that is within thy gates" (Exodus 20:8-10).

God gave the Sabbath commandment to Israel, highlighting its significance in their covenant relationship. However, this commandment was not meant to be exclusive to Israel; it served as a model for how all of humanity should honor the Sabbath.

Inclusion of Gentiles

The prophets foretold that Gentiles would also be brought into God's covenant people, participating in the blessings of the Sabbath.

"Also the sons of the stranger, that join themselves to the Lord, to serve him, and to love the name of the Lord, to be his servants, every one that keepeth the sabbath from polluting it, and taketh hold of my covenant; Even them will I bring to my holy mountain, and make them joyful in my house of prayer" (Isaiah 56:6-7).

This prophecy indicates that Gentiles who join themselves to the Lord and keep the Sabbath are welcomed into God's covenant. The Sabbath is not limited to ethnic Israelites but is open to all who choose to follow God.

The Church: Israelites and Gentiles Grafted In

The New Testament further affirms that both Israelites and Gentiles are part of God's covenant people. The Apostle Paul uses the metaphor of grafting to explain this inclusion.

"And if some of the branches be broken off, and thou, being a wild olive tree, wert grafted in among them, and with them partakest of the root and fatness of the olive tree; Boast not against the branches. But if thou boast, thou bearest not the root, but the root thee" (Romans 11:17-18).

Believers in Jesus, whether Israelites or Gentiles, are grafted into the same spiritual olive tree. This inclusion means that the blessings and responsibilities, including the Sabbath, apply to all members of the Church.

Chapter Four:
How Jesus Kept the Sabbath

The observance of the Sabbath is deeply embedded in Israelite tradition and scriptural commandment. When Jesus walked the earth, He adhered to this practice, not only observing the Sabbath but also teaching about its true purpose. This chapter delves into how Jesus kept the Sabbath, offering insights into His actions and teachings that reveal the deeper significance of this holy day.

Jesus' Observance of the Sabbath

Jesus, born into an Israelite family, grew up practicing the Sabbath as commanded in the Torah. His regular participation in Sabbath customs is evident throughout the Gospels.

"And he came to Nazareth, where he had been brought up: and, as his custom was, he went into the synagogue on the sabbath day, and stood up for to read" (Luke 4:16).

This passage indicates that Jesus habitually attended synagogue services on the Sabbath, where He engaged in reading and teaching the Scriptures. His presence in the synagogue underscores His commitment to the communal and worship aspects of the Sabbath.

Teaching and Healing on the Sabbath

One of the most significant aspects of Jesus' Sabbath observance was His emphasis on teaching and healing. Through His actions, Jesus demonstrated the Sabbath's true purpose as a day of mercy, restoration, and liberation.

"And they went into Capernaum; and straightway on the sabbath day he entered into the synagogue, and taught" (Mark 1:21).

Jesus often chose the Sabbath as a time to teach about the kingdom of God, using this day to reach out to the people with His message. His teachings were transformative, offering new insights into God's will and the essence of the law.

Healing on the Sabbath

Jesus performed many of His healings on the Sabbath, challenging the prevailing legalistic interpretations and highlighting the day's intended purpose of compassion and restoration.

"And, behold, there was a man which had his hand withered. And they asked him, saying, Is it lawful to heal on the sabbath days? that they might accuse him. And he said unto them, What man shall there be among you, that shall have one sheep, and if it fall into a pit on the sabbath day, will he not lay hold on it, and lift it out? How much then is a man better than a sheep?

Wherefore it is lawful to do well on the sabbath days. Then saith he to the man, Stretch forth thine hand. And he stretched it forth; and it was restored whole, like as the other" (Matthew 12:10-13).

In this instance, Jesus emphasizes the principle that doing good and showing mercy are entirely appropriate on the Sabbath. His healing of the man's withered hand illustrates that the Sabbath should be a day for bringing wholeness and relief to those in need.

Redefining the Sabbath

Through His actions and teachings, Jesus redefined the Sabbath, shifting the focus from rigid adherence to rules toward the underlying intent of the commandment. He highlighted that the Sabbath was made for humanity's benefit.

"And he said unto them, The sabbath was made for man, and not man for the sabbath: Therefore the Son of man is Lord also of the sabbath" (Mark 2:27-28).

By declaring Himself Lord of the Sabbath, Jesus asserted His authority to interpret its true meaning. He taught that the Sabbath should be a blessing, not a burden, emphasizing rest, renewal, and acts of kindness.

Confrontations with Religious Leaders

Jesus' approach to the Sabbath often brought Him into conflict with the religious leaders of His time, who had strict interpretations of what constituted acceptable Sabbath activities. These confrontations underscored the tension between legalistic observance and the spirit of the law.

"And it came to pass also on another sabbath, that he entered into the synagogue and taught: and there was a man whose right hand was withered. And the scribes and Pharisees watched him, whether he would heal on the sabbath day; that they might find an accusation against him" (Luke 6:6-7).

Jesus challenged the Pharisees' restrictive rules by healing the man with the withered hand, demonstrating that acts of mercy and necessity were in keeping with God's original intent for the Sabbath.

The Sabbath as a Day of Liberation

Jesus' healings on the Sabbath were also symbolic of the broader liberation He came to bring. They pointed to the ultimate rest and freedom found in Him.

"And ought not this woman, being a daughter of Abraham, whom Satan hath bound, lo, these eighteen years, be loosed from this bond on the sabbath day?" (Luke 13:16).

In healing the woman bound by a disabling spirit, Jesus highlighted the Sabbath's role in setting people free from physical and spiritual bondage. This act of liberation aligns with the Sabbath's deeper purpose as a day of rest and freedom, reflective of God's deliverance.

Lessons for Believers Today

Jesus' example and teachings on the Sabbath provide valuable lessons for believers today:

1. **Prioritize Mercy and Compassion**: Like Jesus, believers are called to prioritize acts of mercy and compassion on the Sabbath. This can involve helping those in need, visiting the sick, or engaging in other acts of kindness.
2. **Focus on Worship and Renewal**: Jesus regularly attended synagogue and taught on the Sabbath, emphasizing the importance of worship and spiritual renewal. Believers should dedicate time to worship, prayer, and reflection on this day.
3. **Embrace Rest**: The Sabbath is a gift of rest. Jesus demonstrated that rest and healing are integral to the Sabbath's observance. Believers should embrace the opportunity to rest from their labors and recharge physically and spiritually.
4. **Reflect God's Love**: Jesus' healings on the Sabbath reflect God's love and desire for human flourishing. Believers are called to

reflect this love by using the Sabbath to build up and support others.

Chapter Five:
What Day is the Sabbath?

The question of when to observe the Sabbath has
been a subject of much discussion and interpretation
throughout history. Traditionally, among the
Israelites, the Sabbath begins at sundown on Friday
and ends at sundown on Saturday. This practice
stems from the biblical understanding of days
beginning at sunset, as detailed in the creation
narrative in Genesis. This chapter explores the
biblical basis for the timing of the Sabbath, the
traditional observance among Israelites, and
considerations for modern observance.

The Biblical Basis for the Sabbath Timing

The concept of the Sabbath as a day of rest originates
in the creation account in Genesis, where God
Himself rests on the seventh day after six days of
creation.

**"Thus the heavens and the earth were finished,
and all the host of them. And on the seventh day
God ended his work which he had made; and he
rested on the seventh day from all his work which
he had made. And God blessed the seventh day,
and sanctified it: because that in it he had rested
from all his work which God created and made"**
(Genesis 2:1-3).

The description of the creation days in Genesis follows the pattern of evening to morning:

"And God called the light Day, and the darkness he called Night. And the evening and the morning were the first day" (Genesis 1:5).

This pattern is repeated for each day of creation, establishing the biblical precedent for reckoning days from evening to evening. Therefore, the seventh day, the Sabbath, follows this same pattern, beginning at sundown on the sixth day and ending at sundown on the seventh day.

Traditional Observance Among Israelites

In Hebrew tradition, the observance of the Sabbath from sundown Friday to sundown Saturday is firmly rooted in biblical commandment and practice. This tradition is based on passages from the Torah that define the Sabbath and its observance.

"Remember the sabbath day, to keep it holy. Six days shalt thou labour, and do all thy work: But the seventh day is the sabbath of the Lord thy God: in it thou shalt not do any work, thou, nor thy son, nor thy daughter, thy manservant, nor thy maidservant, nor thy cattle, nor thy stranger that is within thy gates" (Exodus 20:8-10).

The commandment to observe the Sabbath on the seventh day is clear, and Hebrew tradition has maintained this practice faithfully. The specific timing from sundown to sundown is also supported by Levitical law:

"It shall be unto you a sabbath of rest, and ye shall afflict your souls: in the ninth day of the month at even, from even unto even, shall ye celebrate your sabbath" (Leviticus 23:32).

This passage underscores the understanding that a day in biblical terms runs from evening to evening.

Consistent Seventh-Day Observance

While the traditional observance of the Sabbath from Friday sundown to Saturday sundown is widely practiced, the principle of keeping the Sabbath consistently every seventh day is of paramount importance. The specific day of the week is less significant than the regular, faithful observance of a day of rest and worship every seventh day.

In various parts of the world and throughout different cultures, Christians have adapted their Sabbath observance to fit local calendars and customs. The essential aspect is the consistent, dedicated time set apart for rest and spiritual reflection, in keeping with the biblical commandment.

The Sabbath in the New Testament

The New Testament does not prescribe a specific day for Sabbath observance, but it reinforces the principle of regular rest and worship. Jesus and His disciples observed the Sabbath according to Israelite custom, participating in Temple services and engaging in acts of mercy and healing.

"And he came to Nazareth, where he had been brought up: and, as his custom was, he went into the synagogue on the sabbath day, and stood up for to read" (Luke 4:16).

The apostle Paul also observed the Sabbath, often using it as an opportunity to teach and share the gospel.

"And Paul, as his manner was, went in unto them, and three sabbath days reasoned with them out of the scriptures" (Acts 17:2).

While the early church began to gather on the first day of the week, often referred to as the Lord's Day, in commemoration of Jesus' resurrection, the principle of setting apart regular time for worship and rest remained central.

Modern Considerations for Sabbath Observance

In contemporary practice, Sabbath observance varies. Many groups and individuals continue to observe the Sabbath from Friday sundown to Saturday sundown, following the traditional biblical pattern. Others have adapted other days to keep as their seventh day rest.

The key element is the faithful observance of a day dedicated to God, marked by rest from regular labor and focused on spiritual renewal. Whether this occurs on Saturday, Sunday, or another consistent seventh day, the heart of the Sabbath is found in its purpose rather than its precise timing.

Chapter Six:
Preparation Day

The concept of the Preparation Day is integral to the observance of the Sabbath. Known in Hebrew as "Erev Shabbat," the day before the Sabbath is a time designated for preparing all that is necessary to ensure that the Sabbath is kept holy and free from labor.

Biblical Foundations of Preparation Day

The idea of a Preparation Day is rooted in biblical instruction and tradition. In the Torah, we find the first explicit mention of this practice in the context of gathering manna in the wilderness:

"And it came to pass, that on the sixth day they gathered twice as much bread, two omers for one man: and all the rulers of the congregation came and told Moses. And he said unto them, This is that which the Lord hath said, To morrow is the rest of the holy sabbath unto the Lord: bake that which ye will bake to day, and seethe that ye will seethe; and that which remaineth over lay up for you to be kept until the morning" (Exodus 16:22-23).

This passage highlights the importance of preparing in advance to avoid work on the Sabbath. Gathering twice the amount of manna ensured that the people had enough to sustain them without violating the Sabbath by gathering food.

Jesus and the Preparation Day

The New Testament also mentions the Preparation Day, particularly in the context of Jesus' crucifixion and burial. The Gospels note that Jesus was buried hastily because the Sabbath was approaching:

"When the even was come, because it was the preparation, that is, the day before the sabbath, Joseph of Arimathaea, an honourable counsellor, which also waited for the kingdom of God, came, and went in boldly unto Pilate, and craved the body of Jesus" (Mark 15:42-43).

This reference underscores the cultural and religious importance of the Preparation Day, as even significant events such as the burial of Jesus were conducted in a manner that honored the coming Sabbath.

Practical Observance of Preparation Day

To properly observe the Sabbath, believers need to utilize the Preparation Day effectively. Here are some practical steps for preparing:

1. **Household Chores and Cooking**: Complete household chores such as cleaning, laundry, and cooking before sundown on Friday. Prepare meals that can be easily served

28

without extensive preparation on the Sabbath.

2. **Spiritual Preparation**: Set aside time for spiritual reflection and prayer. Review the week, seek forgiveness for any shortcomings, and prepare your heart for a day dedicated to God.

3. **Errands and Shopping**: Finish all necessary errands and shopping to avoid commercial activities on the Sabbath. Ensure that all essential supplies are in place.

4. **Family Preparation**: Involve the whole family in preparation activities. Teach children the significance of the Sabbath and the importance of getting ready in advance.

5. **Setting the Atmosphere**: Create a peaceful and holy environment in the home. Light candles, play worship music, and set the table in a way that honors the Sabbath.

The Spiritual Significance of Preparation Day

Preparation Day is not just about physical readiness but also spiritual preparedness. It is a time to transition from the busyness of the week to the sanctity of the Sabbath. The intentionality of preparation reflects a heart dedicated to honoring God's commandment and entering His rest.

"Thus the heavens and the earth were finished, and all the host of them. And on the seventh day God ended his work which he had made; and he

rested on the seventh day from all his work which he had made. **And God blessed the seventh day, and sanctified it: because that in it he had rested from all his work which God created and made"** (Genesis 2:1-3).

By preparing diligently, believers align themselves with God's example, emphasizing the holiness of the Sabbath and the importance of rest.

Addressing Common Challenges

Observing the Preparation Day can be challenging in a fast-paced world. Here are some strategies to overcome common obstacles:

1. **Time Management**: Plan the week to ensure that Friday is less hectic. Allocate specific times for preparation activities to avoid last-minute rushes.
2. **Involving Others**: Delegate tasks to family members or roommates. Shared responsibility makes preparation more manageable and fosters a sense of community.
3. **Balancing Work and Preparation**: For those with demanding jobs, try to adjust work schedules to allow for earlier preparation. Discuss the importance of the Sabbath with employers if necessary.
4. **Consistency**: Make Preparation Day a consistent practice. Over time, it will become

a natural and integral part of the weekly routine.

Chapter Seven:
Sabbath Rules

The Sabbath, a day of rest and holiness, is rich with guidance and instruction, deeply rooted in biblical law and exemplified in the book of Nehemiah. Understanding the do's and don'ts of Sabbath observance helps believers align their practices with God's intentions for this sacred day.

Biblical Do's for the Sabbath

1. **Rest from Work** The primary commandment for the Sabbath is to cease from regular labor and rest, following God's example at creation.

   "Six days shalt thou labour, and do all thy work: But the seventh day is the sabbath of the Lord thy God: in it thou shalt not do any work" (Exodus 20:9-10).

2. **Worship and Fellowship** The Sabbath is a day dedicated to the Lord, marked by communal worship and spiritual reflection.

   "Remember the sabbath day, to keep it holy" (Exodus 20:8).

The early Christians gathered for worship and teaching on the Sabbath, emphasizing its role in spiritual community.

"And upon the first day of the week, when the disciples came together to break bread, Paul preached unto them" (Acts 20:7).

3. **Acts of Mercy and Goodness** Jesus demonstrated that the Sabbath is a day for doing good and showing mercy, emphasizing compassion and kindness.

   "Wherefore it is lawful to do well on the sabbath days" (Matthew 12:12).

4. **Family and Community Time** The Sabbath provides an opportunity for families and communities to spend quality time together, fostering relationships and unity. This should primarily be done among other Sabbath keepers who stay within the spirit of what the Sabbath day is about. It's not a day to talk about bills and worldly affairs that non-Sabbath keepers may want to talk about.

   "For the son of man is Lord even of the sabbath day" (Matthew 12:8).

5. **Reflection and Spiritual Growth** Setting aside time for personal reflection, prayer, and study of Scripture helps deepen one's faith and understanding of God.

Biblical Don'ts for the Sabbath

1. **Avoid Regular Work** The most explicit command is to refrain from daily labor and commercial activities.

   "In it thou shalt not do any work, thou, nor thy son, nor thy daughter, thy manservant, nor thy maidservant, nor thy cattle, nor thy stranger that is within thy gates" (Exodus 20:10).

2. **Do Not Engage in Buying and Selling** Commercial activities are to be avoided to keep the day focused on rest and spiritual matters.

   "In those days saw I in Judah some treading wine presses on the sabbath, and bringing in sheaves, and lading asses; as also wine, grapes, and figs, and all manner of burdens, which they brought into Jerusalem on the sabbath day: and I testified against them in the day wherein they sold victuals" (Nehemiah 13:15).

3. **Refrain from Burden-Bearing** Carrying burdens or engaging in laborious tasks is prohibited to maintain the sanctity and restful nature of the day.

   "Thus saith the Lord; Take heed to yourselves, and bear no burden on the

sabbath day, nor bring it in by the gates of Jerusalem; Neither carry forth a burden out of your houses on the sabbath day, neither do ye any work, but hallow ye the sabbath day, as I commanded your fathers" (Jeremiah 17:21-22).

4. **Avoid Travel** Excessive travel or journeys that take away from the restful and reflective nature of the Sabbath are discouraged.

"But pray ye that your flight be not in the winter, neither on the sabbath day" (Matthew 24:20)

Lessons from Nehemiah

Nehemiah provides a powerful example of enforcing Sabbath observance during the rebuilding of Jerusalem. His actions demonstrate the importance of maintaining the sanctity of the Sabbath and the community's commitment to God's laws.

"In those days saw I in Judah some treading wine presses on the sabbath, and bringing in sheaves, and lading asses; as also wine, grapes, and figs, and all manner of burdens, which they brought into Jerusalem on the sabbath day: and I testified against them in the day wherein they sold victuals" (Nehemiah 13:15).

Nehemiah confronted those who violated the Sabbath by engaging in commercial activities and labor. His leadership included practical measures to ensure compliance with the Sabbath laws:

1. **Rebuking Violators** Nehemiah did not hesitate to rebuke those who were desecrating the Sabbath by engaging in commerce and labor.

   "Then I contended with the nobles of Judah, and said unto them, What evil thing is this that ye do, and profane the sabbath day?" (Nehemiah 13:17).

2. **Closing the Gates** To prevent merchants from entering the city and conducting business on the Sabbath, Nehemiah ordered the gates of Jerusalem to be shut before the Sabbath began and not to be opened until it ended.

   "And it came to pass, that when the gates of Jerusalem began to be dark before the sabbath, I commanded that the gates should be shut, and charged that they should not be opened till after the sabbath: and some of my servants set I at the gates, that there should no burden be brought in on the sabbath day" (Nehemiah 13:19).

3. **Stationing Guards** Nehemiah stationed guards at the gates to ensure that no goods were brought in or out, reinforcing the prohibition of commerce.

"So the merchants and sellers of all kind of ware lodged without Jerusalem once or twice. Then I testified against them, and said unto them, Why lodge ye about the wall? if ye do so again, I will lay hands on you. From that time forth came they no more on the sabbath" (Nehemiah 13:20-21).

Practical Applications for Modern Observance

Modern believers can draw from these biblical principles to observe the Sabbath in ways that honor God and reflect its intended purpose. Here are some practical applications:

1. **Plan Ahead** Prepare meals and complete necessary chores before the Sabbath begins to minimize labor and distractions.
2. **Limit Technology Use** Consider setting aside electronic devices and reducing screen time to focus on rest, worship, and family.
3. **Engage in Worship** Attend church services, participate in communal worship, and engage in spiritual activities that draw you closer to God.
4. **Rest and Rejuvenate** Use the Sabbath to rest physically, mentally, and emotionally. Engage in activities that rejuvenate your spirit and body. It's a good day to take a nap.
5. **Spend Time with Loved Ones** Dedicate time to Sabbath keeping family and friends,

strengthening relationships and creating a sense of community.

6. **Reflect and Pray** Set aside time for personal reflection, prayer, and study of Scripture, deepening your spiritual life.

Chapter Eight:
The Covenant of Rest

The dawn of the Sabbath morning brought a serene stillness to the land of Israel. Birds sang gently, and the golden light of the sun bathed the hills and valleys in a divine glow. In homes across the nation, families awoke to a day set apart, a day unlike any other in its holiness and purpose. The Sabbath was not merely a cessation of labor but a profound covenant between God and His people.

"Speak thou also unto the children of Israel, saying, Verily my sabbaths ye shall keep: for it is a sign between me and you throughout your generations; that ye may know that I am the Lord that doth sanctify you" (Exodus 31:13).

The Covenant Established

The roots of the Sabbath are intricately tied to the covenant God made with the people of Israel. This covenant was not only a legalistic framework but a relational bond, emphasizing the holiness and faithfulness of God. Through the Sabbath, God reminded His people of His creative power and His deliverance from bondage.

"Wherefore the children of Israel shall keep the sabbath, to observe the sabbath throughout their generations, for a perpetual covenant. It is a sign between me and the children of Israel for ever: for in six days the Lord made heaven and earth, and on the seventh day he rested, and was refreshed" (Exodus 31:16-17).

The Sabbath was a sign, a perpetual reminder that Israel was a nation set apart for God's purposes. It reinforced their identity and called them to remember their origins and destiny, shaped by the hand of the Almighty.

The Gift of Rest

The command to keep the Sabbath was not intended to be a burden but a gift. In a world where rest was often a luxury and not a right, God mandated a day of rest for everyone—masters, servants, strangers, and even animals. This was a radical concept in the ancient world, highlighting God's concern for the well-being of all His creation.

"But the seventh day is the sabbath of the Lord thy God: in it thou shalt not do any work, thou, nor thy son, nor thy daughter, thy manservant, nor thy maidservant, nor thy cattle, nor thy stranger that is within thy gates" (Exodus 20:10).

This divine rest was a profound equalizer, breaking down societal barriers and fostering a sense of community and shared humanity. It was a day to cease striving, to acknowledge that life and provision ultimately come from God, not from human effort.

The Sabbath in the Wilderness

As the Israelites journeyed through the wilderness, the Sabbath took on additional layers of meaning. It became a test of their trust in God's provision. When manna was given as their daily bread, they were instructed to gather a double portion on the sixth day, for none would be provided on the Sabbath.

"And Moses said, Eat that to day; for to day is a sabbath unto the Lord: to day ye shall not find it in the field. Six days ye shall gather it; but on the seventh day, which is the sabbath, in it there shall be none" (Exodus 16:25-26).

This experience taught the Israelites reliance on God and underscored the Sabbath as a time to rest in His promises. It was a tangible lesson in faith, reminding them that God was their ultimate provider and sustainer.

Christ's Fulfillment of the Sabbath

Centuries later, the teachings and actions of Jesus Christ would bring a deeper understanding of the Sabbath's true essence. Jesus did not come to abolish the Sabbath but to fulfill its purpose and reveal its ultimate meaning. He demonstrated that the Sabbath was made for the benefit of humanity, a day for healing, restoration, and doing good.

"And he said unto them, The sabbath was made for man, and not man for the sabbath: Therefore the Son of man is Lord also of the sabbath" (Mark 2:27-28).

In healing the sick and performing miracles on the Sabbath, Jesus challenged the rigid interpretations of the law and showcased the Sabbath's intent as a day of mercy and compassion. His lordship over the Sabbath signified a new creation, where the burdens of sin and legalism were lifted, offering true rest to all who came to Him.

"Come unto me, all ye that labour and are heavy laden, and I will give you rest. Take my yoke upon you, and learn of me; for I am meek and lowly in heart: and ye shall find rest unto your souls. For my yoke is easy, and my burden is light" (Matthew 11:28-30).

The Early Church and the Sabbath

The early Christian community, while rooted in Hebrew tradition, began to find new ways to honor the Sabbath in light of Christ's resurrection. They continued to gather on the Sabbath for prayer and instruction but also celebrated the first day of the week, Sunday, as the Lord's Day—commemorating Jesus' victory over death.

"And upon the first day of the week, when the disciples came together to break bread, Paul preached unto them, ready to depart on the morrow; and continued his speech until midnight" (Acts 20:7).

This dual observance reflected the early Church's recognition of both the old and new covenants. The Sabbath remained a day of rest and worship, while Sunday became a symbol of new beginnings and eternal hope.

The Covenant Continues

As the Church of Christ grew and spread across different cultures and lands, the observance of the Sabbath and the Lord's Day evolved, but the underlying principles remained unchanged. The Sabbath, as a covenant of rest, continues to call believers to a rhythm of life that honors God, fosters community, and provides spiritual and physical renewal.

In a world increasingly driven by ceaseless activity and material pursuits, the Sabbath stands as a divine invitation to pause, reflect, and find true rest in God. It is a weekly reminder of His sovereignty, His provision, and His love—a sign of the everlasting covenant that He established with His people.

"There remaineth therefore a rest to the people of God. For he that is entered into his rest, he also hath ceased from his own works, as God did from his" (Hebrews 4:9-10).

As we continue to explore the depths of the Sabbath, let us embrace this sacred covenant, allowing its rhythms to shape our lives and draw us closer to the heart of God. Let it be a testament to our faith, a source of strength and renewal, and a foretaste of the eternal rest that awaits in His presence.

Chapter Nine:
The Blessings

In a world driven by relentless productivity and constant activity, the concept of setting aside one day for rest and worship may seem counterintuitive. However, the Sabbath is not just a day off; it is a divine gift, a source of profound blessings for those who faithfully observe it.

Biblical Promises and Blessings

God's commandments regarding the Sabbath come with promises of blessings for those who honor this holy day. These promises are rooted in Scripture, highlighting the spiritual, physical, and communal benefits of Sabbath observance.

"If thou turn away thy foot from the sabbath, from doing thy pleasure on my holy day; and call the sabbath a delight, the holy of the Lord, honourable; and shalt honour him, not doing thine own ways, nor finding thine own pleasure, nor speaking thine own words: Then shalt thou delight thyself in the Lord; and I will cause thee to ride upon the high places of the earth, and feed thee with the heritage of Jacob thy father: for the mouth of the Lord hath spoken it" (Isaiah 58:13-14).

This passage from Isaiah underscores the profound joy and spiritual elevation that come from honoring the Sabbath. God promises delight, spiritual renewal, and a deepened relationship with Him for those who keep the Sabbath holy.

Rest and Renewal

One of the most immediate blessings of the Sabbath is the gift of rest. In a culture that often glorifies busyness and overwork, the Sabbath offers a countercultural rhythm of rest and renewal.

"Come unto me, all ye that labour and are heavy laden, and I will give you rest. Take my yoke upon you, and learn of me; for I am meek and lowly in heart: and ye shall find rest unto your souls. For my yoke is easy, and my burden is light" (Matthew 11:28-30).

Jesus' invitation to find rest in Him is closely tied to the spirit of the Sabbath. By setting aside one day each week, believers can experience physical rest, mental relaxation, and spiritual rejuvenation.

Trusting God's Provision

Observing the Sabbath requires faith in God's provision. It is a weekly exercise in trusting that God will meet our needs, even if we take a break from our labors.

"Therefore I say unto you, Take no thought for your life, what ye shall eat, or what ye shall drink; nor yet for your body, what ye shall put on. Is not the life more than meat, and the body than raiment? Behold the fowls of the air: for they sow not, neither do they reap, nor gather into barns; yet your heavenly Father feedeth them. Are ye not much better than they?" (Matthew 6:25-26).

By keeping the Sabbath, we acknowledge that our ultimate provider is God, not our own efforts. This act of faith allows us to release our anxieties about work and provision, trusting in God's care and timing.

Walking by Faith, Not by Sight

The practice of Sabbath observance aligns with the biblical principle of walking by faith and not by sight.

"For we walk by faith, not by sight" (2 Corinthians 5:7).

In a world that values tangible results and immediate gratification, the Sabbath calls believers to a deeper trust in God's unseen promises. It is a reminder that our value and success are not measured solely by our productivity, but by our obedience and faithfulness to God.

Lessons from Chik-Fil-A

A modern example of the blessings of Sabbath observance can be seen in the business practices of Chik-Fil-A. The fast-food chain is famously closed on Sundays, a decision rooted in the founder's Christian faith and commitment to honoring the Sabbath.

Despite being closed one day a week, Chik-Fil-A has experienced remarkable success and growth. This decision has not only provided employees with a guaranteed day of rest but has also fostered a strong company culture and customer loyalty. The company's success demonstrates that honoring the Sabbath can lead to tangible blessings, even in the competitive business world.

Communal and Familial Blessings

The Sabbath also brings blessings to families and communities. By setting aside regular time for rest and worship, families can strengthen their relationships and create lasting memories. Communities of faith can gather to support and encourage one another, fostering a sense of unity and belonging.

"And let us consider one another to provoke unto love and to good works: Not forsaking the assembling of ourselves together, as the manner of some is; but exhorting one another: and so

much the more, as ye see the day approaching"
(Hebrews 10:24-25).

The communal aspect of the Sabbath helps build a strong, supportive network of relationships that are crucial for spiritual and emotional well-being.

Chapter Ten:
Setting Boundaries

Observing the Sabbath in a world that does not share the same commitment to this sacred day can be challenging. Setting boundaries, especially in interactions with non-Sabbath keepers, is crucial for maintaining the sanctity and restfulness of the Sabbath.

Understanding the Importance of Boundaries

The purpose of the Sabbath is to provide rest and renewal, allowing believers to focus on their relationship with God and their spiritual well-being. To protect this time, it is essential to set boundaries that prevent intrusion from the demands and distractions of everyday life.

"Remember the sabbath day, to keep it holy. Six days shalt thou labour, and do all thy work: But the seventh day is the sabbath of the Lord thy God: in it thou shalt not do any work" (Exodus 20:8-10).

By clearly defining what activities are permissible on the Sabbath and communicating these boundaries to others, believers can create a space that honors God and fosters true rest.

Establishing Personal Boundaries

1. **Define Sabbath Activities**: Determine which activities align with the purpose of the Sabbath. This might include attending worship services, spending time in prayer and Bible study, resting, and enjoying quality time with family.
2. **Plan Ahead**: Prepare for the Sabbath by completing chores, errands, and work responsibilities beforehand. This preparation helps minimize the need for work-related tasks during the Sabbath.
3. **Limit Technology Use**: Consider reducing or eliminating the use of electronic devices that could distract from the restful and worshipful nature of the day.
4. **Set Clear Expectations**: Clearly communicate your Sabbath observance to friends, family, and colleagues. Let them know which activities you will not be participating in and why.

Communicating Boundaries to Non-Sabbath Keepers

1. **Be Honest and Respectful**: Explain your Sabbath observance and the reasons behind it honestly and respectfully. Use this as an opportunity to share your faith and the importance of the Sabbath.
2. **Seek Understanding**: Encourage others to understand and respect your commitment,

even if they do not share the same beliefs. This mutual respect can help prevent misunderstandings and conflicts.

3. **Offer Alternatives**: If friends or family invite you to activities that conflict with your Sabbath observance, suggest alternative times or activities that do not interfere with the Sabbath.

4. **Use Scripture**: Share relevant Bible verses that highlight the importance of the Sabbath and God's command to keep it holy.

"If thou turn away thy foot from the sabbath, from doing thy pleasure on my holy day; and call the sabbath a delight, the holy of the Lord, honourable; and shalt honour him, not doing thine own ways, nor finding thine own pleasure, nor speaking thine own words" (Isaiah 58:13).

Handling Work and Social Obligations

1. **Inform Your Employer**: If possible, discuss your Sabbath observance with your employer and request accommodation. Many employers are willing to respect religious observances if they are informed in advance.

2. **Set Boundaries with Colleagues**: Politely decline work-related tasks or meetings scheduled during your Sabbath. Offer to complete these tasks before or after the Sabbath.

3. **Respectfully Decline Invitations**: If social events or gatherings conflict with your

Sabbath, explain your observance and suggest rescheduling or participating in a way that aligns with your boundaries.

Maintaining Boundaries

1. **Stay Firm but Flexible**: While it is important to be firm in your commitment to the Sabbath, be flexible and gracious in your interactions with others. Understand that not everyone will immediately understand or respect your boundaries.
2. **Seek Support**: Connect with a community of fellow Sabbath keepers who can provide support, encouragement, and accountability.
3. **Evaluate and Adjust**: Regularly evaluate your Sabbath observance and boundaries. Make adjustments as needed to ensure that the day remains restful and spiritually enriching.

Biblical Examples of Setting Boundaries

Nehemiah's leadership provides a powerful example of setting boundaries to protect the sanctity of the Sabbath. When he saw that the people were violating the Sabbath by engaging in commerce, he took decisive action to restore proper observance.

"In those days saw I in Judah some treading wine presses on the sabbath, and bringing in sheaves, and lading asses; as also wine, grapes, and figs, and all manner of burdens, which they brought

into Jerusalem on the sabbath day: and I testified against them in the day wherein they sold victuals" (Nehemiah 13:15).

Nehemiah's actions included closing the city gates to prevent merchants from entering and conducting business on the Sabbath.

"And it came to pass, that when the gates of Jerusalem began to be dark before the sabbath, I commanded that the gates should be shut, and charged that they should not be opened till after the sabbath: and some of my servants set I at the gates, that there should no burden be brought in on the sabbath day" (Nehemiah 13:19).

His firm stance helped the community return to proper Sabbath observance and honor God's command.

Trusting God's Provision

Setting boundaries for the Sabbath requires faith in God's provision and care. Trusting that God will meet your needs, even as you set aside one day for rest and worship, is an exercise in walking by faith.

"Therefore take no thought, saying, What shall we eat? or, What shall we drink? or, Wherewithal shall we be clothed? (For after all these things do the Gentiles seek:) for your heavenly Father knoweth that ye have need of all these things. But seek ye first the kingdom of God, and his

righteousness; and all these things shall be added unto you" (Matthew 6:31-33).

Believers can find peace and confidence in knowing that God honors their commitment to the Sabbath and will provide for their needs.

Chapter Eleven:
The Sabbath and Community

As the believers settled into the rhythm of their Sabbath retreat, they were reminded of the profound impact the Sabbath had on community life. This day, set apart by God, was not only for individual rest and reflection but also for fostering relationships and strengthening the bonds within the community. The Sabbath was a time for communal worship, shared meals, and collective rejoicing, encapsulating the essence of a holy and unified people.

The Communal Aspect in Israel

In ancient Israel, the Sabbath was a communal event. Families and neighbors gathered together to worship God and to enjoy each other's company. The Sabbath rituals were performed in the home and the Temples, creating a rhythm that brought the community together in worship and rest.

"Ye shall keep my sabbaths, and reverence my sanctuary: I am the Lord" (Leviticus 19:30).

The temple became the center of Sabbath observance. Here, the Israelites gathered to hear the

Torah read and expounded. It was a time for learning, singing psalms, and offering prayers, reinforcing the communal identity as God's chosen people. This shared experience helped to knit the community together, fostering a sense of belonging and mutual support.

Jesus and the Sabbath Community

Jesus Christ, during His ministry, often engaged with the community on the Sabbath. He attended synagogues, taught, and healed, emphasizing the relational and restorative nature of the Sabbath. His actions demonstrated that the Sabbath was a time for doing good and for uplifting one another.

"And he came to Nazareth, where he had been brought up: and, as his custom was, he went into the synagogue on the sabbath day, and stood up for to read" (Luke 4:16).

In healing the sick and performing miracles on the Sabbath, Jesus highlighted the importance of compassion and mercy within the community. His approach challenged the rigid interpretations of the law and reoriented the focus towards love and service.

"And, behold, there was a man which had his hand withered. And they asked him, saying, Is it lawful

to heal on the sabbath days? that they might accuse him. And he said unto them, What man shall there be among you, that shall have one sheep, and if it fall into a pit on the sabbath day, will he not lay hold on it, and lift it out? How much then is a man better than a sheep? Wherefore it is lawful to do well on the sabbath days" (Matthew 12:10-12).

The Early Church and Shared Fellowship

The early Christian church continued the tradition of communal Sabbath observance while also introducing new practices that reflected their faith in the risen Christ. Believers gathered in homes to break bread, share the Scriptures, and pray together. These gatherings were not just about rest but about strengthening the bonds of faith and fellowship.

"And they continued stedfastly in the apostles' doctrine and fellowship, and in breaking of bread, and in prayers. And all that believed were together, and had all things common" (Acts 2:42, 44).

This communal aspect was crucial for the early Christians, who often faced persecution and needed the support and encouragement of their fellow believers. The Sabbath gatherings provided a refuge, a place to renew their strength and reaffirm their commitment to Christ and each other.

A Modern Sabbath Community

In contemporary times, the Sabbath continues to offer a unique opportunity for building community. Despite the relentless pace of modern life, the Sabbath provides a sacred pause, inviting people to come together in worship and fellowship. It is a time to disconnect from the distractions of the world and to reconnect with God and one another.

In the small retreat nestled in the forest, the believers gathered in a circle, sharing their experiences and reflections. They prayed together, sang hymns, and read from the Scriptures, finding solace and strength in their shared faith. The sense of community was palpable, a testament to the enduring power of the Sabbath to bring people together.

The Power of Shared Rest

The communal observance of the Sabbath fosters a deep sense of unity and shared purpose. It reminds believers that they are part of a larger story, connected not just by faith but by the rhythm of life ordained by God. The Sabbath is a time to celebrate these connections, to build relationships, and to support one another in their spiritual journeys.

"Behold, how good and how pleasant it is for brethren to dwell together in unity!" (Psalm 133:1).

As the day progressed, the believers participated in communal activities that emphasized rest and joy. They shared meals, walked in nature, and engaged in conversations that uplifted their spirits. The Sabbath was a gift, a time to relish the beauty of God's creation and the warmth of fellowship.

Chapter Twelve:
The Sabbath and Creation

The serene forest retreat provided an ideal setting for the believers to contemplate the deep connections between the Sabbath and the natural world. Surrounded by the beauty of God's creation, they were reminded of the foundational role the Sabbath played in the rhythm of the universe, as established by God Himself at the beginning of time.

The Creation Sabbath

The Sabbath's origins are rooted in the very act of creation. After six days of creative work, God instituted the seventh day as a day of rest, setting a divine precedent for the rhythm of work and rest.

"Thus the heavens and the earth were finished, and all the host of them. And on the seventh day God ended his work which he had made; and he rested on the seventh day from all his work which he had made. And God blessed the seventh day, and sanctified it: because that in it he had rested from all his work which God created and made" (Genesis 2:1-3).

God's rest on the seventh day was not due to weariness but was a deliberate act of sanctification, marking the day as holy and setting it apart from the other days. This divine rest imbued the Sabbath with a sense of completion and wholeness, reflecting the perfection of God's creation.

The Sabbath and Environmental Stewardship

The command to observe the Sabbath extends beyond human rest and includes a call to care for the land and all living creatures. In the Torah, this principle is evident in the instructions for the Sabbatical year and the Year of Jubilee, which promote sustainable practices and environmental stewardship.

"And six years thou shalt sow thy land, and shalt gather in the fruits thereof: But the seventh year thou shalt let it rest and lie still; that the poor of thy people may eat: and what they leave the beasts of the field shall eat. In like manner thou shalt deal with thy vineyard, and with thy oliveyard" (Exodus 23:10-11).

By allowing the land to rest every seventh year, the Israelites were acknowledging their dependence on God and demonstrating respect for the natural world. This practice prevented the exploitation of the earth's resources and ensured that the land could rejuvenate, benefiting both people and wildlife.

Jesus and the Restoration of Creation

Jesus Christ, in His ministry, often highlighted the interconnectedness of the Sabbath and creation. His miracles, many performed on the Sabbath, were acts of restoration that reflected the original harmony of Eden. By healing the sick and feeding the hungry on the Sabbath, Jesus was restoring creation to its intended state of wholeness and balance.

"The Spirit of the Lord is upon me, because he hath anointed me to preach the gospel to the poor; he hath sent me to heal the brokenhearted, to preach deliverance to the captives, and recovering of sight to the blind, to set at liberty them that are bruised, To preach the acceptable year of the Lord" (Luke 4:18-19).

Jesus' proclamation of the "acceptable year of the Lord" alludes to the Year of Jubilee, reinforcing the connection between Sabbath rest and the restoration of creation. His ministry brought glimpses of the ultimate redemption and renewal that would come through His sacrificial work.

The Early Church and Creation Care

The early Christian community continued to uphold the Sabbath's principles of rest and stewardship. They recognized that honoring the Sabbath included caring for creation and living sustainably. This understanding was part of their broader call to love God and neighbor, extending that love to all of God's creation.

"For the earnest expectation of the creature waiteth for the manifestation of the sons of God. For the creature was made subject to vanity, not willingly, but by reason of him who hath subjected the same in hope, Because the creature itself also shall be delivered from the bondage of corruption into the glorious liberty of the children of God" (Romans 8:19-21).

The apostle Paul's words remind us that creation itself longs for liberation and restoration. The early Church's commitment to living in harmony with creation was a testimony to their hope in the ultimate redemption of all things through Christ.

A Modern Call to Creation Care

In the modern era, the call to observe the Sabbath and care for creation is more urgent than ever. Environmental degradation, climate change, and the exploitation of natural resources pose significant threats to the health of our planet. Observing the Sabbath offers a countercultural practice that challenges these destructive patterns and promotes sustainable living.

"And God saw every thing that he had made, and, behold, it was very good. And the evening and the morning were the sixth day" (Genesis 1:31).

God's declaration of creation as "very good" reminds us of the inherent value and beauty of the natural world. Observing the Sabbath encourages us to pause, appreciate, and protect this divine gift. It calls us to adopt practices that honor the Creator by preserving the integrity of His creation.

Practical Steps for Sabbath Observance and Creation Care

As the believers at the forest retreat contemplated their role as stewards of creation, they discussed practical steps for integrating Sabbath principles into their daily lives. Here are some ways to honor the Sabbath through environmental stewardship:

1. **Rest from Consumption:** Embrace the Sabbath as a day to minimize consumption and reduce waste. Avoid shopping and unnecessary use of resources, focusing instead on activities that replenish and renew.

2. **Engage with Nature:** Spend time in nature to appreciate its beauty and reflect on God's creation. Activities such as hiking, gardening, or simply sitting outdoors can deepen your connection with the natural world.

3. **Support Sustainable Practices:** Make choices that support sustainability, such as buying locally produced food, reducing energy consumption, and advocating for policies that protect the environment.

4. **Educate and Advocate:** Educate yourself and others about environmental issues and advocate for change in your community. Join efforts to protect natural habitats and support initiatives that promote environmental justice.

5. **Practice Gratitude:** Cultivate a spirit of gratitude for the gifts of creation. Use the Sabbath as a time to thank God for the

beauty and abundance of the natural world
and to recommit to its care.

Chapter Thirteen:
Neglecting the Sabbath

The Sabbath is a day ordained by God for rest, worship, and reflection. It is a time set apart to honor the Creator and renew our spiritual and physical strength. However, neglecting the Sabbath can have serious consequences, both spiritually and communally.

Biblical Warnings and Consequences

The Bible contains numerous warnings about the importance of keeping the Sabbath and the consequences of failing to do so. God's displeasure with Sabbath neglect is clear, and His responses to such disobedience are stern and unequivocal.

"But if ye will not hearken unto me to hallow the sabbath day, and not to bear a burden, even entering in at the gates of Jerusalem on the sabbath day; then will I kindle a fire in the gates thereof, and it shall devour the palaces of Jerusalem, and it shall not be quenched" (Jeremiah 17:27).

In this passage, God warns the Israelites that neglecting the Sabbath would lead to severe punishment, including the destruction of their city. This demonstrates the serious nature of Sabbath observance and the dire consequences of disregarding it.

Spiritual Consequences

Neglecting the Sabbath results in spiritual ramifications that affect one's relationship with God. The Sabbath is a sign of the covenant between God and His people, and disregarding it signifies a breach of this sacred relationship.

"Moreover also I gave them my sabbaths, to be a sign between me and them, that they might know that I am the Lord that sanctify them. But the house of Israel rebelled against me in the wilderness: they walked not in my statutes, and they despised my judgments, which if a man do, he shall even live in them; and my sabbaths they greatly polluted: then I said, I would pour out my fury upon them in the wilderness, to consume them" (Ezekiel 20:12-13).

This passage from Ezekiel illustrates that failure to keep the Sabbath results in a breakdown of sanctification and a severance from God's blessings. It highlights how Sabbath observance is integral to maintaining a holy and dedicated life to God.

Physical and Emotional Burnout

The Sabbath is designed to provide rest and rejuvenation. Ignoring this day of rest can lead to physical exhaustion and emotional burnout.

Continuous work without a designated period for rest can deplete one's energy and productivity, ultimately affecting overall well-being.

God, in His wisdom, instituted the Sabbath to ensure that His creation would have regular intervals of rest. By not observing the Sabbath, individuals miss out on the restorative benefits that God intended for them.

Communal and Societal Impact

The Sabbath is not only a personal observance but also a communal one. When a community collectively honors the Sabbath, it strengthens social bonds and fosters a sense of unity and shared purpose. Conversely, when the Sabbath is neglected, the community loses an essential aspect of its identity and cohesion.

In Nehemiah, we see how neglecting the Sabbath had broader societal implications:

"In those days saw I in Judah some treading wine presses on the sabbath, and bringing in sheaves, and lading asses; as also wine, grapes, and figs, and all manner of burdens, which they brought into Jerusalem on the sabbath day: and I testified against them in the day wherein they sold victuals" (Nehemiah 13:15).

Nehemiah's actions show that Sabbath neglect led to economic activities overshadowing spiritual

70

observance, disrupting the communal sanctity and leading to a need for correction and reform.

Loss of Blessings

Keeping the Sabbath comes with promised blessings, and neglecting it leads to the forfeiture of these blessings. God promises joy, provision, and spiritual renewal to those who honor the Sabbath.

"If thou turn away thy foot from the sabbath, from doing thy pleasure on my holy day; and call the sabbath a delight, the holy of the Lord, honourable; and shalt honour him, not doing thine own ways, nor finding thine own pleasure, nor speaking thine own words: Then shalt thou delight thyself in the Lord; and I will cause thee to ride upon the high places of the earth, and feed thee with the heritage of Jacob thy father: for the mouth of the Lord hath spoken it" (Isaiah 58:13-14).

This passage highlights the rich blessings that come from observing the Sabbath. Neglecting it means missing out on the joy and spiritual nourishment that God has promised.

Hardening of the Heart

Repeatedly ignoring the Sabbath can lead to a hardened heart, making it difficult to respond to God's guidance and correction. The Israelites experienced this when they continually disregarded God's commands, including the Sabbath.

"But my people would not hearken to my voice; and Israel would none of me. So I gave them up unto their own hearts' lust: and they walked in their own counsels" (Psalm 81:11-12).

When people refuse to keep the Sabbath, they risk becoming more resistant to God's voice and direction, leading to spiritual waywardness and separation from God's will.

In ancient Israel, failing to keep the Sabbath was not just a personal neglect but a communal violation that could lead to being cast out from the nation. This severe consequence underscored the gravity of the Sabbath commandment. God's law stipulated strict adherence to the Sabbath, and persistent disobedience could result in being cut off from the community.

"Ye shall keep the sabbath therefore; for it is holy unto you: every one that defileth it shall surely be put to death: for whosoever doeth any work therein, that soul shall be cut off from among his people" (Exodus 31:14).

This verse highlights the seriousness with which Sabbath observance was treated, equating its neglect with actions warranting the severest punishments, including death or exile. Being cast out of Israel for not keeping the Sabbath served as a stark warning and a means of preserving the nation's sanctity and faithfulness to God's covenant. It emphasized that communal cohesion and divine blessing were deeply intertwined with honoring the Sabbath.

One Year of Sabbath Bible Study Topics (52 Weeks)

Bible Study Topics

1. **Creation**: Explore the creation narrative in Genesis 1-2.
2. **The Fall of Man**: Study Genesis 3 and its implications for humanity.
3. **The Flood and Noah**: Learn about God's judgment and covenant with Noah in Genesis 6-9.
4. **The Patriarchs**: Investigate the lives of Abraham, Isaac, and Jacob in Genesis 12-50.
5. **The Exodus**: Study the story of Israel's deliverance from Egypt in Exodus 1-14.
6. **The Ten Commandments**: Examine the giving of the law at Mount Sinai in Exodus 20 and Deuteronomy 5.
7. **The Tabernacle**: Learn about the construction and significance of the tabernacle in Exodus 25-40.
8. **The Conquest of Canaan**: Study Joshua's leadership and the conquest of Canaan in the book of Joshua.
9. **The Judges**: Explore the era of the judges in the book of Judges.
10. **Ruth and Redemption**: Study the story of Ruth and Boaz.

11. **The Rise of the Monarchy**: Investigate the lives of Saul, David, and Solomon in 1 Samuel, 2 Samuel, and 1 Kings.
12. **The Divided Kingdom**: Learn about the split between Israel and Judah in 1 Kings 12 and the subsequent history.
13. **The Prophets**: Study the messages of major and minor prophets (Isaiah, Jeremiah, Ezekiel, Daniel, Hosea, etc.).
14. **The Exile and Return**: Explore the Babylonian exile and the return to Jerusalem in Ezra and Nehemiah.
15. **The Wisdom Literature**: Study the books of Job, Psalms, Proverbs, Ecclesiastes, and Song of Solomon.
16. **The Gospels**: Examine the life, teachings, miracles, and parables of Jesus in Matthew, Mark, Luke, and John.
17. **The Sermon on the Mount**: Study Jesus' teachings in Matthew 5-7.
18. **The Parables of Jesus**: Explore the parables and their meanings in the Gospels.
19. **The Miracles of Jesus**: Study the miracles performed by Jesus.
20. **The Passion of Christ**: Learn about the events of Jesus' crucifixion, burial, and resurrection in the Gospels.
21. **The Acts of the Apostles**: Study the early church and the spread of the Gospel in Acts.
22. **The Epistles of Paul**: Explore the teachings of Paul in Romans, Corinthians, Galatians, Ephesians, Philippians, Colossians,

Thessalonians, Timothy, Titus, and Philemon.

23. **The General Epistles**: Study the letters of James, Peter, John, and Jude.
24. **The Book of Revelation**: Investigate the apocalyptic vision and its implications.
25. **The Fruit of the Spirit**: Learn about the fruit of the Spirit in Galatians 5:22-23.
26. **The Armor of God**: Study the spiritual armor in Ephesians 6:10-18.
27. **Prayer**: Explore the teachings on prayer throughout the Bible (Matthew 6:5-15, Philippians 4:6-7).
28. **Faith and Works**: Study the relationship between faith and works in James 2.
29. **The Nature of God**: Explore God's attributes and character.
30. **The Trinity**: Study the concept of the Trinity and its biblical foundations.
31. **Salvation**: Learn about the doctrine of salvation and its implications.
32. **Sanctification**: Study the process of becoming more like Christ.
33. **The Kingdom of God**: Explore Jesus' teachings on the Kingdom of God.
34. **Discipleship**: Study what it means to be a disciple of Christ.
35. **Christian Ethics**: Explore biblical teachings on morality and ethics.
36. **Love**: Study the biblical definition and importance of love (1 Corinthians 13, 1 John 4).

37. **Grace and Mercy**: Explore the concepts of grace and mercy throughout the Bible.
38. **The End Times**: Study biblical prophecies about the end times and the return of Christ.
39. **The Role of the Church**: Learn about the purpose and function of the church.
40. **Spiritual Gifts**: Study the spiritual gifts listed in 1 Corinthians 12 and Romans 12.
41. **Stewardship**: Explore biblical principles of stewardship and giving.
42. **The Beatitudes**: Study the blessings pronounced by Jesus in Matthew 5:1-12.
43. **The New Covenant**: Learn about the new covenant established by Jesus.
44. **Christian Living**: Explore practical instructions for living a Christian life (Romans 12, Ephesians 4-6).
45. **Forgiveness**: Study the biblical teachings on forgiveness.
46. **Suffering and Perseverance**: Explore the Bible's teachings on suffering and perseverance.
47. **Joy and Contentment**: Study biblical principles of joy and contentment.
48. **Justice and Righteousness**: Explore the themes of justice and righteousness in the Bible.
49. **The Nature of Sin**: Study the origin and consequences of sin.
50. **The Resurrection**: Learn about the resurrection of Jesus and its significance.
51. **The Second Coming**: Study biblical teachings on the second coming of Christ.

52. **Eternal Life**: Explore the Bible's promises of eternal life and the hope of heaven.